ANIMAL TRACKS
of the
Southeast States

by Chris Stall

D0912011

Virginia, Kentucky, Tennessee, North
Carolina, South Carolina, Georgia, Florida,
Alabama, Mississippi, Louisiana, and
Arkansas

THE MOUNTAINEERS/SEATTLE

*To Lainey in Atlanta, and to Donna and Eveline in Orchard Park
at Mulege, Baja California Sur.*

The Mountaineers: Organized 1906 " . . . to explore, study, preserve, and enjoy
the natural beauty of the Northwest."

© 1989 by The Mountaineers
All rights reserved

2 1 0 9
5 4 3 2 1

Published by The Mountaineers
306 Second Avenue West, Seattle, Washington 98119

Published simultaneously in Canada by Douglas & McIntyre, Ltd.,
1615 Venables Street, Vancouver, B.C. V5L 2H1

Manufactured in the United States of America

Book design by Betty Watson
Cover design by Nick Gregoric
Track on cover: Wild boar

Library of Congress Cataloging in Publication Data

Stall, Chris.
    Animal tracks of the Southeast : Virginia, Kentucky, Tennessee,
North Carolina, South Carolina, Georgia, Florida, Alabama,
Mississippi, Louisiana, and Arkansas / by Chris Stall.
      p.   cm.
    Includes bibliographical references.
    ISBN 0-89886-223-X
    1. Animal tracks—Southern States. 2. Mammals—Southern States.
3. Birds—Southern States. I. Title.
QL768.S733 1989
599.0975—dc20
                                        89-38141
                                         CIP

CONTENTS

Preface

Most people don't get a chance to observe the animals in the wild, with the exceptions of road kills and a few nearly tame species in parks and campgrounds. Many wild animals are nocturnal or scarce, and many are shy and secretive to avoid the attention of predators, or stealthy as they stalk their next meal. In addition, most wild creatures are extremely wary of humans either instinctively or because they've learned through experience to be that way. We may catch fortuitous glimpses now and then, but few of us have the time or motivation required for lengthy journeys into wild country for the sole purpose of locating animals. The result is that areas where we would expect to see animals often seem practically devoid of wildlife.

That's rarely the case, of course. Actually, many animals reside in or pass through all reasonably wild habitats. Though we may not see them, they nevertheless leave indications of their passage. But for the most part such signs are obscure or confusing so that only the most experienced and knowledgeable wilderness travelers notice them.

There's one grand exception: *animal tracks.* Often readily apparent even to the most casual and inexperienced observer, tracks not only indicate the presence of wild animals but can also be matched relatively easily with the animals that made them. I guess that's why I have been fascinated by animal tracks since my childhood in rural New York, and why that focus has continued through two decades of wandering and searching for them in wild lands all across North America.

Animal Tracks of the Southeast is a compilation of many years and many miles of my own field work, protracted observations, sketching, photography, and research into a list of articles and books too long to name and too heavy to carry into the backcountry.

Animal tracks may be something you concern yourself with only when you happen on them, or your interest in tracks may become nearly obsessive. You may find yourself hiking with your chin resting securely on your chest, feverishly scanning the ground for clues. You may seek out snow because tracks show up on it better than most other surfaces. In the absence of snow, you might find yourself altering your routes, avoiding bedrock and ground cover, seeking out damp sand, soft dirt and mud along streams, near ponds and lakes, around swamps. You may journey into the desert in early morning, before the sand dries and moves on the wind. After a rainfall, you might make special trips to check fresh mud, even along dirt roads or hiking trails, knowing that among evidence of human activity the animal prints will be clear and precise.

Whatever your degree of interest, I hope you will enjoy using this book, in your backyard or in the wildest and most remote regions of the Southeast region, and that your interest in identifying tracks grows until you reach the level of knowledge at which you no longer need this book.

Good luck!

Chris Stall
Mulege, Baja California Sur, Mexico

Introduction

HOW TO USE THIS BOOK

1. When you first locate an unknown track, look around the immediate area to locate the clearest imprint (see Tracking Tips below). You can usually find at least one imprint or even a partial print distinct enough for counting toes, noting the shape of the heel pad, determining the presence or absence of claw marks, and so on.

2. Decide what kind of animal is most likely to have made the tracks; then turn to one of the two main sections of this book. The first and largest features mammals; the second, much shorter section is devoted entirely to birds.

3. Measure an individual track, using the ruler printed on the back cover of this book. Tracks of roughly five inches or less are illustrated life-size; those larger than five inches have been reduced as necessary to fit on the pages.

4. Flip quickly through the appropriate section until you find tracks

that are about the same *size* as your mystery tracks. The tracks are arranged roughly by size from smallest to largest.

5. Search carefully for the tracks in the size range that, as closely as possible, match the *shape* of the unknown tracks.

6. If you find the right shape but the size depicted in the book is too big, remember that the illustrations represent tracks of an average *adult* animal. Perhaps your specimen was made by a young animal. Search some more: on the ground nearby you might locate the tracks of a parent, which will more closely match the size of the illustration.

7. Read the comments on range, habitat, and behavior, to help confirm the identification.

This book is intended to assist you in making field identifications of commonly encountered animal tracks. To keep the book compact, my remarks are limited to each animal's most obvious characteristics. By all means enhance your own knowledge of these track makers. Libraries and book stores are good places to begin learning more about wild animals. Visits to zoos with southeastern wildlife on display can also be worthwhile educational experiences. And there's no substitute for firsthand field study. You've found tracks, now you know what animals to look for. Read my notes on diet, put some bait out, sit quietly downwind with binoculars for a few hours, and see what comes along. Or follow the tracks awhile. Use your imagination and common sense, and you'll be amazed at how much you can learn, and how rewarding the experiences can be.

As you use this book, remember that track identification is an inexact science. The illustrations in this book represent average *adult* tracks on *ideal* surfaces. But many of the tracks you encounter in the wild will be those of smaller-than-average animals, particularly in late spring and early summer. There are also larger-than-average animals, and injured or deformed ones, and animals that act unpredictably. Some creatures walk sideways on occasion. Most vary their gait so that in a single set of tracks, front prints may fall ahead, behind, or beneath the rear. In addition, ground conditions are usually less than ideal in the wild, and animals often dislodge debris, which may further confuse the picture. Use this book as a guide, but anticipate lots of variations.

In attempting to identify tracks, remember that their size can vary greatly depending on the type of ground surface—sand that is loose or firm, wet or dry; a thin layer of mud over hard earth; deep soft mud; various lightly frozen surfaces; firm or loose dirt; dry or moist snow; a dusting of snow or frost over various surfaces; and so on. Note the surface from which the illustrations are taken and interpret what you find in nature accordingly.

You should also be aware that droplets from trees, windblown debris, and the like often leave a variety of marks on the ground that could be mistaken for animal tracks. While studying tracks, look around for and be aware of non-animal factors that might have left "tracks" of their own.

The range notes pertain only to the states of Virginia, Kentucky, Tennessee, North Carolina, South Carolina, Georgia, Florida, Alabama, Mississippi, Louisiana and Arkansas. Many trackmakers in this book also live elsewhere in North America. Range and habitat remarks are general guidelines because both are subject to change, from variations in both animal and human populations, climatic factors, pollution levels, acts of God, and so forth.

The size, height, and weight listed for each animal are those for average adults. Size refers to length from nose to tip of tail; height, the distance from ground to shoulder.

A few well-known species have been left out of this book: moles and bats, for example, which leave no tracks. Animals that may be common elsewhere but are rare, or occur only in the margins of the Southeast have also been omitted. Some species herein, particularly small rodents and birds, stand as representatives of groups of related species. In such cases the featured species is the one most commonly encountered and widely distributed. Related species, often with similar tracks, are listed in the notes. Where their tracks can be distinguished, guidelines for doing so are provided.

If you encounter an injured animal or an apparently orphaned infant, you may be tempted to take it home and care for it. Do not do so. Instead, report the animal to local authorities, who are better able to care for it. In addition, federal and state laws often strictly control the handling of wild animals. This is always the case with species classified as *rare* or *endangered*. Animals are better left in the wild, and to do otherwise may be illegal.

TRACKING TIPS

At times you'll be lucky enough to find a perfectly clear and precise track that gives you all the information you need to identify the maker with a quick glance through this book. More often the track will be imperfect or fragmented. Following the tracks may lead you to a more readily identifiable print. Or maybe you have the time and inclination to follow an animal whose identity you already know in order to learn more about its habits, characteristics, and behavior.

Here are some tips for improving your tracking skills:

1. If you don't see tracks, look for disturbances—leaves or twigs in unnatural positions, debris or stones that appear to have been moved or turned. Stones become bleached on top over time, so a stone with its darker side up or sideways has recently been dislodged.

2. Push small sticks into the ground to mark individual signs. These will help you keep your bearings and "map out" the animal's general direction of travel.

3. Check immovable objects like trees, logs, and boulders along the route of travel for scratches, scuff marks, or fragments of hair.

4. Look at the ground from different angles, from standing height, from kneeling height and, if possible, from an elevated position in a tree or on a boulder or rise.

5. On very firm surfaces, place your cheek on the ground and observe the surface, first through one eye, then the other, looking for unnatural depressions or disturbances.

6. Study the trail from as many different directions as possible. Trail signs may become obvious as the angle of light between them and your eyes changes, especially if dew, dust, or rain covers some parts of the ground surface.

7. Check for tracks beneath recently disturbed leaves or fallen debris.

8. Try not to focus your attention so narrowly that you lose sight of the larger patterns of the country around you.

9. Keep your bearings. Some animals circle back if they become aware of being followed. If you find yourself following signs in a circular path, try waiting motionless and silent for a while, observing behind you.

10. Look ahead as far as possible as you follow signs. Animals take the paths of least resistance, so look for trails or runways. You may even catch sight of your quarry.

11. Animals are habitual in their movements between burrows, den sites, sources of water and wood, temporary shelters, prominent trees, and so on. As you track and look ahead, try to anticipate where the creature might be going.

12. Stalk as you track; move as carefully and quietly as possible.

The secrets to successful tracking are patience and knowledge. Whenever you see an animal leaving tracks, go look at them and note the activity you observed. When you find and identify tracks, make little sketches alongside the book's illustrations, showing cluster patterns, or individual impressions that are different from those drawn. Make notes about what you learn in the wilds and from other readings. Eventually, you will build a body of knowledge from your own experience, and your future attempts at track identification will become easier and more certain.

This book is largely a compilation of the author's personal experiences. Your experiences with certain animals and their tracks may be identical, similar, or quite different. If you notice a discrepancy or find tracks that are not included in this book, carefully note your observations, or even amend the illustrations or text to reflect your own experiences. This book is intended for use in the field as a tool for identifying animal tracks of the Southeast.

Mammals
Invertebrates
Amphibians
Reptiles

INVERTEBRATES

The smallest track impressions you are likely to encounter in nature will probably look something like those illustrated at the right.

From left to right, the illustration shows tracks of two common varieties of beetle, a centipede, and finally a cricket. The track of an earthworm crosses from lower left to the upper right corner, as well.

You might initially mistake insect marks for a variety of scuffs and scratches left by windblown or otherwise dislodged debris, the imprint of raindrops that have fallen from overhanging limbs, impressions left by the smallest mice, or even the perplexing calligraphy of toads. If you have more than a square foot or so of ground surface to scrutinize, however, you will usually find that insect tracks form a recognizably connected line; the extremely shallow depth of the trail of imprints is also a good clue that a very lightweight being has passed by.

With literally millions of species out there, trying to identify the insect that made a particular track can be challenging, but there are times when you can follow a trail and find, at the end, either the bug itself, or a burrow which could yield its resident with a little patient and careful excavation on your part. If you spend enough time in one area, you will begin to observe specific species in the act of making their tracks, and that, as with animal tracks in general, goes a long way toward track recognition.

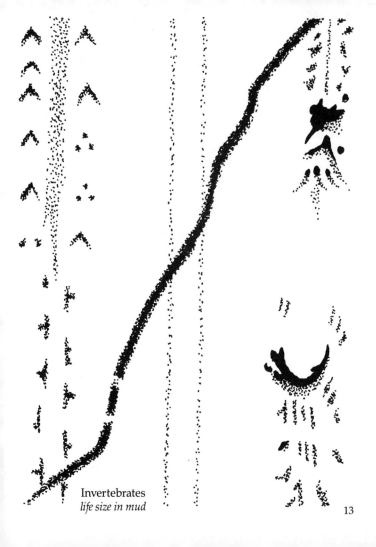

Invertebrates
life size in mud

13

EASTERN HARVEST MOUSE   *Reithrodontomys humulis*

Order: Rodentia (gnawing mammals). **Family:** Cricetidae (New World rats and mice). **Range and habitat:** throughout all southern states except most of Arkansas and northern Louisiana; in lowland fields, brush areas, broom sedges and briar patches. **Size and weight:** 7 inches; less than an ounce. **Diet:** seeds and young plant sprouts. **Sounds:** faint, clear, high-pitched bugling sounds.

The eastern harvest mouse is a small, grayish-brown mouse with a pale gray or buff underside. Its most distinguishing trait is the apple-sized nest it builds either on the ground or in bushes, using twigs, moss, bird feathers and other soft available materials. The mouse then stores surplus food items in its globular haven.

Oldfield, white-footed, cotton, Texas, Florida, golden, and Fulvous harvest mice share range, habitat, and many of the characteristics of the eastern harvest mouse. Most of these similar species can, in fact, only be told apart by differences in teeth or bone structure.

Tracks of these tiny mice are, at best, difficult to locate and to distinguish from a variety of other dimples and scrapes on the earth's surface. If you are fortunate enough to find a clear set of tracks, they may resemble those illustrated at the right.

Eastern Harvest Mouse
life size in mud

SOUTHERN RED-BACKED VOLE *Clethrionomys gapperi*
Boreal vole, gapper redback vole, red-backed mouse

Order: Rodentia (gnawing mammals). **Family:** Cricetidae (New World mice and rats). **Range and habitat:** in Allegheny Mountains, Virginia to North Carolina; in forested areas, preferably damp environments. **Size and weight:** 6 inches; 1 ounce. **Diet:** primarily vegetarian, including berries, herbs, nuts, seeds, lichens, and fungi; occasionally insects. **Sounds:** rarely audible to humans.

Voles, out and about by day, can frequently be glimpsed scurrying around. Though mouselike in habits, voles are squatter and plumper than mice, with no obvious neck and a slightly shorter and bushier tail. They are active year round, day and night, and are good climbers. Of all the voles present within the southern states, the southern red-backed vole is the only one with an easily distinguishable characteristic, its reddish back.

Several voles and volelike animals in the region, including the rock, prairie, and woodland voles, and the southern bog lemming, occupy ranges that overlap that of the red-backed vole and so closely resemble it (and one another) that positive identification of the animals, or their tracks, is practically impossible in the field.

Vole tracks are generally distinctive as a group because vole feet are peculiarly shaped and voles tend to walk and sit rather than run and leap like mice. Southern red-backed voles usually travel on the surface, while meadow voles generally live in denser vegetation and burrow along intricate systems of runways, which they often carefully line with cuttings of grass. Then again, southern red-backed voles occasionally do that also. Walking pairs of red-backed vole tracks will be only an inch or so apart, with no tail marks. Other vole tracks are more mouselike, with 2 to 4 print clusters about 3 to 6 inches apart. Meadow and yellownose voles have slightly longer tails than the others, which may leave drag marks occasionally.

Southern Red-backed Vole
life size in mud

SOUTHERN SHORT-TAILED SHREW   *Blarina carolinensis*

Order: Insectivora (insect-eating mammals, including shrews, moles, and bats). **Family:** Soricidae (shrews). **Range and habitat:** throughout the Southeast; primarily in forests at lower elevations. **Size and weight:** 5 inches; 1 ounce. **Diet:** slugs, snails, spiders, insects, and larvae; occasionally mice and carrion. **Sounds:** commonly silent.

Shrews are vole-shaped creatures, but with shorter legs, a slightly more elongated body, and a long pointed snout. *All* shrews are little eating machines, though, with extremely high metabolism, evidenced by heartbeat and respiration rates around 1200 per minute. In fact, shrews consume more than their own body weight in food on a daily basis.

The shrews' constant and aggressive quest for food makes their tracks, in general, fairly easy to identify. The animals move around with more single-minded purpose than mice or voles, usually in a series of short hops in which the rear feet fall over the tracks of the front feet; the tails often drag, leaving the distinctive pattern shown, usually less than an inch in width. When individual impressions are more distinct, you may notice that shrews have five toes on both fore- and hind feet (most micelike creatures have four toes on the forefeet).

Eight shrew species live around the Southeast, all with similar habits and track patterns. Shrew dentists have a big advantage in distinguishing the various species because differences in unicuspid teeth are all that differentiate many of them.

Southern Short-tailed Shrew
life size in snow

MEADOW JUMPING MOUSE   *Zapus hudsonius*

Order: Rodentia (gnawing mammals). **Family:** Zapodidae (jumping mice). **Range and habitat:** from Kentucky and Virginia south to northeast Georgia; widespread and adaptable, prefers low, lush grassy areas and damp meadows near water, but may be found anywhere. **Size and weight:** 9 inches; 1 ounce. **Diet:** vegetarian, including grasses, seeds, berries, and fungi. **Sounds:** frequent chirps at night between members of foraging groups.

The meadow jumping mouse varies in color from pale buff to rust, with a very long tail and relatively large, strong hind legs and feet. It is not easy to sight in the wild because it is generally nocturnal during warm weather and hibernates during the winter. You are most likely to see this little animal crossing the road in the beam of your car headlights.

The tracks of this jumping mouse are quite distinctive and should be easy to identify, even if the imprints are not very clear, because it is the only mouse living in the habitat described above that takes single jumps, or several in a series, of 6 inches to 5 feet each. Rear-foot impressions will be noticeably longer (around half an inch) than those of other similar-sized creatures, and its long tail leaves marks more frequently (either among the footprints or out to the side). But when leaping in a series of bounds, only the hind feet contact the ground, leaving a trail of small, widely spaced print-pairs without tail drag marks, also unique.

These tracks could also be made by the woodland jumping mouse, which lives in the Alleghenies from Virginia to northeast Georgia, in forested areas near water, especially with dense green vegetation.

Meadow Jumping Mouse
life size in mud

SOUTHEASTERN POCKET GOPHER   *Geomys pinetis*

Order: Rodentia (gnawing mammals). **Family:** Geomyidae (pocket gophers). **Range and habitat:** portions of Georgia, Florida and Alabama; in open fields, pasture, and occasionally open woods. **Size and weight:** 11 inches; 6 ounces. **Diet:** various foliage, twigs, bark, roots and tubers. **Sounds:** silent.

The pocket gopher is a peculiar, highly evolved burrowing rodent named for the fur-lined cheek pockets in which it carries both food and nesting materials; the pockets can be turned inside out to empty their contents and for cleaning.

Southeastern pocket gophers look like small buff to grayish rats except that their large, yellowish front teeth are always showing; their lips close behind the teeth, so the animals can gnaw through earth and roots during tunneling without getting dirt in their mouths. Pocket gophers spend most of their lives in extensive tunnel systems. Other signs of pocket-gopher activity include tracks or tooth marks on limbs near their tunnel entrances, and plugged earthen mounds near those entrances.

The tracks are similar in size to those of a chipmunk, but the pocket gopher's elongated heel pads leave larger impressions. The most distinctive characteristic of pocket-gopher tracks, however, is the imprint of five toes on both front and rear feet; the relatively long digging claws on its front feet leave prominent marks, and the distance between the toe and the claw marks is greater than with any other similar-sized creature. Similar tracks could also be made by the plains pocket gopher in portions of Arkansas and Louisiana.

Southeastern Pocket Gopher
life size in mud

MARSH RICE RAT

Oryzomys palustris

Order: Rodentia (gnawing mammals). **Family:** Cricetidae (New World rats and mice). **Range and habitat:** portions of all southern states; near marshes, occasionally drier, grassy areas. **Size and weight:** 14 inches; 2 ounces. **Diet:** aquatic plants including rice where available; also aquatic animals, insects, fungi, fruits. **Sounds:** silent.

The marsh rice rat is a medium-sized grayish-brown rat that usually prefers to live within a system of runways among marsh vegetation. It is an excellent swimmer, often foraging underwater for food items, and leaving remnants of crabs, snails and other shellfish around its feeding platforms made of plant materials bent over water. The marsh rice rat is a generally nocturnal and solitary little beast that you probably will not sight very often.

You might find its tracks, however, in the soft damp earth or mud near its preferred marshy habitat. Tracks similar to those illustrated but located in grassy or weedy fields may have been left by a hispid cotton rat, which overlaps almost the entire range of the marsh rice rat and is about the same size. On Cudjoe Key, such tracks will almost certainly be those of the Key rice rat. As a general rule, however, within the southern states any given habitat might be home to a great variety of similar little mice-like creatures, and the cunning use of a live trap may be the only practical way to determine which species of various young or full-grown voles, mice, and rats is actually leaving tracks in a particular area. Print lengths of up to .8 inches and walking strides of about 2 inches may help to distinguish the larger rats.

Marsh Rice Rat
life size in mud

EASTERN CHIPMUNK   *Tamias striatus*

Order: Rodentia (gnawing mammals). **Family:** Sciuridae (squirrels). **Range and habitat:** Virginia, Kentucky, Tennessee, North and South Carolina, Mississippi and Louisiana; in deciduous forests and fringe areas, also common in parks and camping areas. **Size and weight:** 9 inches; 3 ounces. **Diet:** vegetation, berries, grains and seeds, insects, carrion. **Sounds:** shrill and persistent "chip, chip."

The eastern chipmunk is the only chipmunk species that lives in the Southeast, so you will have no problem identifying this very conspicuous animal with the black and white side-stripes and moderately bushy tail. It chatters nearly constantly, leaping and scurrying over the ground and up and down tree trunks during the daylight hours.

The track clusters of the eastern chipmunk are usually 2 to 2.5 inches in width, with 7 to 15 inches between groups of prints. Chipmunks often run up on their toes, so rear-heel impressions may not show at all or may be less clear. The hind-foot tracks (five-toed) almost always fall closer together than, and in front of, the forefoot tracks (four-toed), typical of all squirrel-family members.

If you find tracks like those described above in midwinter, however, you can assume they were left by a small squirrel rather than a chipmunk, because chipmunks tend to hole up with food caches in cold weather. At any rate, if you are indeed looking down at chipmunk tracks, regardless of season, you will probably catch sight of the maker, because chipmunks are noisy and not all that timid, particularly around areas frequented by people; in fact, they will more than likely approach you for a handout.

Eastern Chipmunk
life size in mud

WOODHOUSE'S TOAD
Bufo woodhousei

Order: Salientia (frogs, toads, and allies). **Family:** Bufonidae (true toads). **Range and habitat:** throughout the southern states except Florida and coastal portions of Georgia and South Carolina; in all moist and adjoining areas, wherever insects are abundant, usually but not necessarily within a mile of permanent dampness. **Size and weight:** 4 inches; 2 ounces. **Diet:** insects. **Sounds:** high-pitched musical trills.

Toads are small, froglike animals with dry, warty skin, in a variety of reddish, brown, and gray colors. They are primarily nocturnal, but can be seen at dawn or dusk, or even by day.

Unlike frogs, toads often travel fairly far from sources of water. They do require water for breeding, however; look for their long, ropy strings of eggs in stagnant pond water.

Individual toad tracks can be confusing and might be mistaken for the tiny dimples and scratchings of tracks left by small mice or insects. A toad tends to sit quietly waiting for insects to fly past it, at which time it takes a few leaps in the direction of the wing noise, snares the bug with its long, sticky tongue, then repeats the procedure. Thus it may change direction of travel abruptly and often, commonly backtracking over earlier prints, which can make a very confusing picture on the ground.

Toad tracks generally consist of nothing more distinct than a trail of little holes and scrapes, with impressions that sometimes resemble little toad hands. The distinguishing characteristics are the mode of wandering, the short rows of four or five round dimples left by the toes of the larger rear feet, and the drag marks often left by the feet as the toad moves forward; those toe-drag marks point in the direction of travel. Similar tracks, from coastal Mississippi east through Florida, Georgia, and North and South Carolina, could have been made by the oak or southern toads, or the American Toad throughout all inland areas.

You won't get warts from handling toads, but make sure you don't have insect repellent or other caustic substances on your hands that might injure the toad's sensitive skin.

28

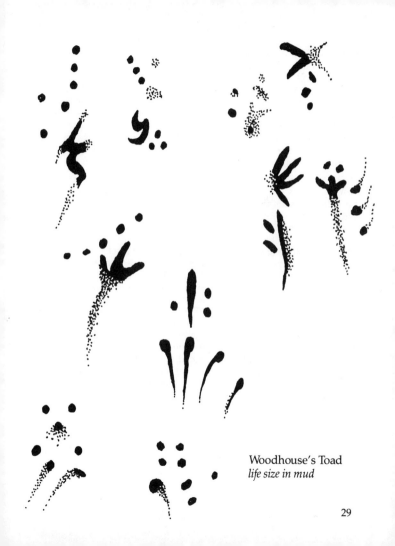

Woodhouse's Toad
life size in mud

29

LONG-TAILED WEASEL
LEAST WEASEL

Mustela frenata
Mustela nivalis

Order: Carnivora (flesh-eating mammals). **Family:** Mustelidae (weasels and skunks). **Range and habitat:** the South except Florida, throughout the Mid-Atlantic states; both weasels frequent most habitats where water is nearby. **Size and weight:** variable, generally averages 14 inches; 10 ounces. **Diet:** small rodents, chipmunks, birds, amphibians. **Sounds:** may shriek or squeal when alarmed or making a kill; also purrs, chatters, hisses.

The long-tailed weasel is an aggressive hunter by day and night, will climb and swim but generally confines its activities to an agile pursuit of prey on the ground, where it also finds various burrows. It grows a white coat with black tail tip in cold-winter regions.

The least weasel, smallest carnivore in North America, is a scaled-down version of the long-tailed weasel. It lives in the Appalachian Mountains, and shares most of the long-tailed weasel's behavior.

Least and long-tailed weasel tracks are difficult to distinguish conclusively. Generally, least weasel track clusters are about 1.5 inches wide and less than 2 feet apart, whereas long-tailed weasel clusters may be as much as 3 inches in width, with leaps of up to 50 inches. But how do you really know whether the tracks were made by a large Least weasel or a small long-tailed weasel?

If close study doesn't reveal fifth toe prints, individual weasel tracks can be tough to distinguish from those of squirrels or rabbits. But weasels usually *alternate* long and short bounds, and leave lines of doubled-over tracks with occasional tail-drag marks, whereas rabbits and squirrels tend to leave four separate prints in each cluster without tail drags. The latter also leave evidence of vegetarian diets, whereas weasels, being carnivores, do not.

Long-tailed Weasel
life size in mud

RED SQUIRREL
Pine squirrel, chickaree

Tamiasciurus hudsonicus

Order: Rodentia (gnawing mammals). **Family:** Sciuridae (squirrels). **Range and habitat:** from Virginia south through the Alleghenies; in coniferous or mixed forests and occasionally nearby in swamp fringes. **Size and weight:** 12 inches; 8 ounces. **Diet:** nuts, fungi, insects, larvae, cones, seeds, and vegetation. **Sounds:** a great variety of noisy, ratchetlike sounds.

The red squirrel is active during the day year round. You often hear one scolding from a low branch before you see the little squirrel. Quite common throughout most of its range, this small, noisy squirrel is easy to identify by its rust or grayish-red coat of fur, fluffy rust-colored tail, and the white rings around its eyes. It lives in ground burrows as well as in downed logs and standing trees and is particularly fond of pine cones, which it shucks for the seeds, leaving piles of cone remnants everywhere. Occasionally in the fall, you may be startled by green cones falling systematically and seemingly unaided from tall coniferous trees. The red squirrel is up there, out of sight, cutting the cones; later it will gather them from the forest floor and hide them away for the cold months to come.

The red squirrel has long, curved toenails that act as hooks for tree climbing and which often leave definite imprints. Clear tracks show the squirrel's four toes on its front feet, and the five toes on its hind feet, which usually fall ahead of the front. Often the heel marks will be absent because the red squirrel is usually running quickly and nervously when it is on the ground; the track spacing may vary widely, with leaps from 8 to 30 inches. Individual prints may be as long as 1.5 inches.

Red Squirrel
life size in mud

NORTHERN FLYING SQUIRREL
SOUTHERN FLYING SQUIRREL

Glaucomys sabrinus
Glaucomys volans

Order: Rodentia (gnawing mammals). **Family:** Sciuridae (squirrels). **Range and habitat:** *G. sabrinus* lives in the Appalachian Mountains; *G. volans* occurs throughout the southern states except in southern Florida; in mixed forests, especially live oak. **Size and weight:** 9–11 inches; 3–5 ounces. **Diet:** bark, fungi, lichen, seeds, insects, eggs, carrion. **Sounds:** generally silent but occasionally makes chirpy, birdlike noises.

Give or take an inch or two and a couple of ounces, the northern and southern flying squirrels are, for all practical purposes, indistinguishable, but since all flying squirrels are nocturnal, all you will likely see of either species is its tracks. That is, unless you happen to knock against or cut down one of the hollow trees in which both species are fond of nesting; in that case, if the squirrel that runs out is a *small* and medium grayish-brown, it's likely you've had a rare glimpse of a flying squirrel.

During summer, flying squirrels don't leave much evidence of their passage. They live mostly in trees, using the fur-covered membrane that extends along each side of the body from the front to the rear legs to glide between trees and occasionally from tree to earth, where they usually leave no marks on the ground cover of their forest habitat. On snow, however, their tracks can be identified because they lead away from what looks like a miniature, scuffed snow-angel, the pattern left when a flying squirrel lands at the end of an aerial descent. The tracks may wander around a bit if the squirrel has foraged for morsels, but they will lead back to the trunk of a nearby tree before long.

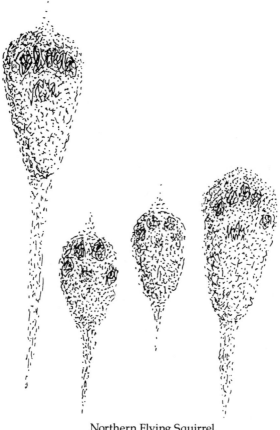

Northern Flying Squirrel
life size in snow

GRAY SQUIRREL

Sciurus carolinensis

Order: Rodentia (gnawing mammals). **Family:** Sciuridae (squirrels). **Range and habitat:** throughout all southern states except the Tampa Bay area of Florida; in hardwood (especially oak) or mixed hardwood–evergreen forests, and occasionally nearby in swamp fringes. **Size and weight:** 20 inches; 1 pound. **Diet:** mostly acorns and cone seeds, also various nuts, fungi, insects and larvae, some vegetation. **Sounds:** variety of rapid, raspy barks.

The large gray squirrel is such a common park animal that most of us are familiar with it. It is normally gray above, with an offwhite belly and long bushy tail. Active all day, year round, the gray squirrel nests in tree cavities or in conspicuous nests made of sticks and shredded bark, usually 20 feet or more above the ground, but spends a lot of time on the ground searching for nuts and seeds and ranges widely around its home trees.

Because of their wandering habits, gray squirrels leave a lot of tracks in areas traveled by other similar-sized animals, and partial track impressions can be confusing. Gray squirrels are often running, so their long rear heels don't leave prints. The real keys to recognizing gray squirrel tracks are the number of toes—four on the front feet and five on the rear—and the track characteristics common to all members of the squirrel family: front tracks close together; parallel impressions of the entire toes often present, rather than just the tips; and the two middle toes of the front feet and three middle toes of the rear feet, almost always close together and lined up ahead of each heel print, with only the outer toes splayed out to the sides. The toes are also relatively farther from the heel pads in squirrel tracks than in weasel-family tracks. If after careful investigation, combined as always with consideration of habitat and pattern of movement, you've determined tracks belong to a squirrel-family member, as opposed to a cottontail, for example, or one of the smaller weasels, then the size of the tracks will distinguish the gray squirrel: front tracks about an inch across: rear tracks less than 2.5 inches long, depending on surface condition and how much of the heel has left an impression; track straddle about 4.5 inches; leaps of 2 to 3 feet.

Gray Squirrel
life size in mud

FOX SQUIRREL

Sciurus niger

Order: Rodentia (gnawing mammals). **Family:** Sciuridae (squirrels). **Range and habitat:** throughout the southern states; in live oak, pine, and mixed forests, also cypress and mangrove swamps. **Size and weight:** 25 inches; 2 to 3 pounds. **Diet:** prefers hickory nuts and acorns, also variety of other nuts, seeds, fungi, berries, bird eggs, bark, buds. **Sounds:** ratchet-like, rapid and raspy barks.

The fox squirrel is the largest tree squirrel in America. It can be distinguished from the gray squirrel by color as well as size: the underside of the fox squirrel is generally more buff than white, and there is more rust and yellowish fur mixed with the gray of its coat, particularly on its tail.

It's very difficult, however, in practical terms, to distinguish between the tracks of the two, because while there is clearly a difference in body size between the two, all adult fox squirrels do not necessarily have larger feet than all adult gray squirrels.

A good clue to the identity of the track maker may be found in wandering and eating patterns rather than track measurements: gray squirrels tend to wander far from their home trees, searching for food, which they often eat where they find it; fox squirrels are more likely to carry edibles back to a favorite feeding perch. So if in following the tracks, you discover a large deposit of food remnants near a log, stump, or branch, the tracks are probably those of a fox squirrel. To be certain, however, you could hang around quietly for a while and see what activity you can observe.

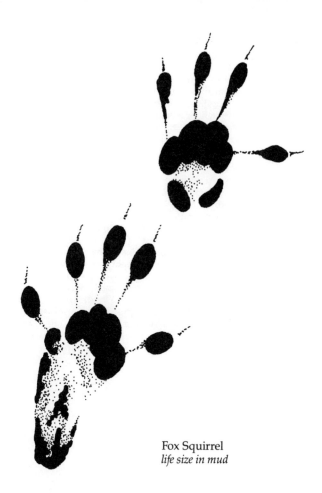

Fox Squirrel
life size in mud

EASTERN WOODRAT
Neotoma floridana
Cave rat, pack rat

Order: Rodentia (gnawing mammals). **Family:** Cricetidae (New World rats and mice). **Range and habitat:** absent from portions of Virginia, North Carolina, eastern Tennessee and southern Florida; among rocky cliffs, hedges and wooded lowlands. **Size and weight:** 15 inches; 12 ounces. **Diet:** vegetarian supplemented with insects, eggs, carrion when available. **Sounds:** occasionally drums and thumps feet.

This native American rat is active year round but it is seldom sighted in the wild, as it is generally nocturnal and frequents rugged terrain. The eastern woodrat is slightly larger than the imported Norway and black rats and has a furry, not scaly, tail. Unlike Norway and black rats, woodrats avoid humans and their habitations, although they may "borrow" shiny and other attractive objects from abandoned buildings or active campsites within their territories.

The eastern woodrat has fairly stubby toes, four on the fore feet and five on the hind, that usually leave uniquely shaped tracks with no claw marks. The tracks are roughly in line when walking and grouped as illustrated when running, with 8 or more inches separating the clusters of prints. Like most small rodents, when woodrats leap, their front feet land first, followed by the back feet which come down ahead of the front imprints, providing the spring into the next leap. If the characteristic stubby-toed imprints are not clear, the short spacing relative to foot size should help distinguish woodrat tracks from similar ones made by other animals of comparable size.

Eastern Woodrat
life size in mud

MINK

Mustela vison

Order: Carnivora (flesh-eating mammals). **Family:** Mustelidae (the weasel family). **Range:** throughout all southern states; in brushy or open forested areas along streams, lakes, and other wetlands. **Size and weight:** 24 inches; 3 pounds. **Diet:** primarily muskrats and smaller mammals; also birds, frogs, fish, crayfish, and eggs. **Sounds:** snarls, squeals, and hisses.

The mink is the sleekest, most exuberant of the weasels, and the most aquatic. About the size of a small cat and medium brown all over, it is an excellent swimmer and may wander several miles a day searching for food along stream- and riverbanks and around the shorelines of lakes. Its den, too, is usually in a stream- or riverbank, an abandoned muskrat nest, or otherwise near water. Generally a nocturnal hunter, its tracks are likely to be the only indication you will have of its presence.

The mink leaves either groups of four tracks like those illustrated or the characteristic double pair of tracks, usually not more than 26 inches apart. The tracks nearly always run along the edge of water. Though it has five toes both front and rear, it is quite common for only four-toed imprints to be apparent. Like all mustelids, the mink employs its scent glands to mark territory; so, as you track it through its hunting ranges, you may notice a strong scent here and there, different but as potent as that of its relative the skunk. You might also, in snow, find signs of prey being dragged, invariably leading to the animal's den.

Mink
life size in mud

43

NINE-BANDED ARMADILLO   *Dasypus novemcinctus*

Order: Edentata (anteaters, sloths, and armadillos). **Family:** Dasypodidae (armadillos). **Range and habitat:** Arkansas, Louisiana, Florida, southern Mississippi, Alabama and Georgia; in woodlands, brushy or rocky areas, primarily in any area where sandy or moist soils encourage easy digging. **Size and weight:** 30 inches; 12 pounds. **Diet:** insects, ants, worms, crayfish, amphibians, bird and reptile eggs, carrion, some vegetation including berries. **Sounds:** nearly incessant pig-like grunting while digging.

Our native armadillo is a nocturnal, big-eared, pointy-nosed, short-legged, heavy-bodied animal with nine transverse bands of gray, bony, segmented hide covering its body like armor plating. Its rump, shoulders, and head are protected by similar horny shields. This interesting animal's range extends as far south as Argentina, but its relatively hairless body makes maintaining body heat difficult, limiting its potential northerly migration. It can swim and run surprisingly quickly, but spends most of its time digging for food and excavating burrows, for which its large, powerful claws and sensitive nose are well adapted. Females annually give birth to identical quadruplets, all developed from a single fertilized egg, which can walk within a few hours of birth.

Armadillo tracks are often obscured by dragging body armor, but a careful search along the trail will usually reveal some reasonably clear tracks, which are quite unique in shape. Particularly if the trail is old or weathered, you will at least find telltale pairs of holes left by the animal's long front claws, which it thrusts into the ground as it goes its stiff-legged way.

Nine-banded Armadillo
life size in sand

45

EASTERN SPOTTED SKUNK
Civet cat, hydrophobia cat

Spilogale putorius

Order: Carnivora (flesh-eating mammals). **Family:** Mustelidae (the weasel family). **Range and habitat:** absent from parts of coastal northeast Florida, Georgia, the Carolinas, and Virginia; in brushy or sparsely wooded areas along streams, among boulders, and in open areas and farmlands. **Size and weight:** 25 inches; 3 pounds. **Diet:** omnivorous, including rats, mice, birds, insects, eggs, carrion, seeds, fruit, and occasionally vegetation. **Sounds:** usually silent.

The spotted skunks are the smallest and most visually interesting of the North American skunks. About the size of a small housecat, with an assortment of white spots and streaks over its black coat, the spotted skunk has finer, silkier fur than the other skunks, is quicker and more agile, and occasionally climbs trees, although it doesn't stay aloft for long. Like all skunks, it is primarily nocturnal, but you might see it at dawn or dusk, or foraging during the daylight in winter, when hunger keeps it active. Skunks have the most highly effective scent glands of all the mustelids and can, when severely provoked, shoot a fine spray of extremely irritating methyl mercaptan as far as 25 feet. Everyone knows what that smells like.

Skunk tracks are all similar, with five toes on each foot leaving prints, toenail prints commonly visible, and front tracks slightly less flat-footed than rear. Spotted skunk tracks will be about 1.25 inches long at most; adult striped skunks leave tracks up to 2 inches in length. On the other hand, the quick spotted skunk leaves a foot or more between *clusters* of prints when running, while the larger striped skunk lopes along with only about 5 or 6 inches between more strung-out track groups.

Because skunks can hold most land animals at bay with their formidable scent, owls are their chief predators. If you are following a skunk trail that ends suddenly, perhaps a bit of black and white fur remaining mysteriously where the tracks disappear, you might be able to guess what transpired.

Eastern Spotted Skunk
life size in mud

MUSKRAT

Ondatra zibethicus

Order: Rodentia (gnawing mammals). **Family:** Cricetidae (New World rats and mice). **Range and habitat:** absent from some southern parts of the Gulf Coast states, all of Florida, and eastern Georgia; in streams, lakes, ponds, and marshes. **Size and weight:** 24 inches; 4 pounds. **Diet:** aquatic vegetation; occasionally shellfish and small aquatic animals. **Sounds:** high-pitched squeaks.

The muskrat is a large brown rat with a volelike appearance, modified for its aquatic life by a rudderlike scaly tail and partially webbed hind feet. Muskrats associate readily with beavers and occasionally nest within the superstructure of beaver lodges. More often, muskrats burrow into riverbanks or construct lodges similar to those of beavers but extending only a couple of feet above water level and composed of aquatic vegetation, primarily grasses and reeds, rather than parts of trees. Muskrat lodges always have underwater entrances. Mainly nocturnal, the muskrat can be seen during the late afternoon or at dusk, pulling the V of its ripples across a still water surface, tail skulling behind, mouth full of grass for supper or nest-building.

Muskrat tracks are nearly always found in mud close to water. The muskrat is one of the few rodents with five toes on its front feet, but its truncated inner toes often leave no imprint. It leaves tracks about 2 inches apart when walking to 12 inches apart when running, with the tail sometimes dragging as well. The track of the hind foot is usually more distinctive than that of the front, and the stiff webbing of hair between the toes is often visible.

Slightly smaller but similar-shaped tracks around marshes of southeast Georgia and Florida indicate the presence of the round-tailed muskrat, a species very similar in shape and characteristics to the muskrat but only two-thirds its size and with, yes, a round tail.

Muskrat
life size in mud

NUTRIA

Myocastor coypus

Order: Rodentia (gnawing mammals). **Family:** Capromyidae (nutrias). **Range and habitat:** Louisiana, Arkansas, and coastal portions of Mississippi, Alabama, Florida, North Carolina and Virginia; in marshes, lakes and ponds, rivers and streams. **Size and weight:** 40 inches; 15 pounds. **Diet:** almost all land and water green plants. **Sounds:** a variety of pig-like grunts at dusk; also splashes loudly when entering water if startled on land.

This large South American rodent was first introduced into Louisiana in the 1930s as a possible fur-bearing animal. The nutria thrived, escaped its farms or was transplanted elsewhere, and rapidly expanded its range. It looks very much like a grayish-brown beaver with a long, hairless, round tail. The nutria is primarily nocturnal and aquatic, with many beaver- and muskrat-like habits; it spends its life in or very near water, employs large floating feeding and resting platforms, excavates burrows in riverbanks or uses various lodges or other nest sites formed and abandoned by beavers or muskrats. Its young are born precocial and can swim with their parents within 24 hours of birth.

Nutria tracks will always be found very near water, usually in conjunction with well-worn trails of flattened undergrowth. An adult's tracks are fairly distinctive; aside from their unique shape, they can be distinguished from beaver tracks by their greater width and more conspicuous evidence of webbing, by the absence of tail drag marks, and lack of felled trees, wood chips, freshly gnawed branches and dragged building materials commonly found in beaver territory. Also, beavers often walk a hundred feet or more from water searching for building materials, but nutria almost never leave the water's immediate proximity. Muskrat tracks, clearly smaller, should never cause confusion.

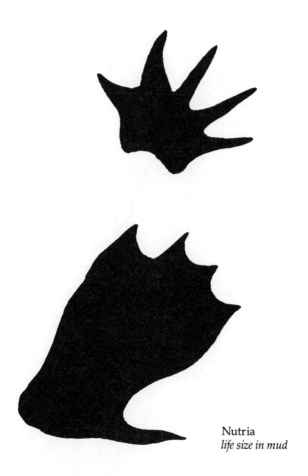

Nutria
life size in mud

BULLFROG

Rana catesbiana

Order: Salientia (frogs, toads, and allies). **Family:** Ranidae (true frogs). **Range and habitat:** throughout the Southeast except southern Florida; in ponds, lakes, marshes and swamps, year-around bodies of water. **Size and weight:** body 5–8 inches, with long legs; 4 ounces. **Diet:** insects. **Sounds:** low-pitched croaks, deep jug-o-rum, especially at dawn and dusk.

Eighty-one species of frogs live north of the Rio Grande, of which the bullfrog is the largest. Varying in color from a mottled darker-gray to green, with an off-white belly, bullfrogs live in or very near water because they must keep their skin wet and they breed in water. They use distinctive vocalizations to signal each other and to attract mates. The 4-to-6-inch-long vegetarian tadpoles take up to two years to transform into carnivorous adults. As with all toads and frogs, be sure your hands are free from insect repellent or other caustic substances before you handle a bullfrog as it has particularly sensitive skin.

Frogs walk or hop in a more plantigrade manner than toads, so their tracks tend to be more easily recognizable. You will commonly find impressions of the full soles of their feet and might even be able to see that their hind feet are webbed, except the last joint of the longest toe, although these delicate membranes don't always imprint. The toed-in imprints of the small front feet combined with a straddle of 5 or 6 inches should leave no doubt about the identity of bullfrog tracks, even if the hind-foot impressions are less than distinct.

Nine other terrestrial frog species live in the southern states, ranging in overall size from 1 to 6 inches. Their tracks are nearly identical to those of the bullfrog, but relatively smaller.

Bullfrog
⅔ life size in mud

LIZARD-LIKE CREATURES
Orders: Caudata (Salamanders)
Squamata (Lizards)
Crocodylia (Crocodiles and Alligators)

Many interesting lizard-like creatures inhabit portions of the southern states, including the potentially dangerous American alligator, the largest reptile in North America, which can be found from southern Arkansas to coastal North Carolina; the tiger salamander, the world's largest terrestrial salamander, absent only from the Appalachians; and a great variety of other newts, salamanders and lizards in a bewildering array of colors, shapes, and sizes from less than 3 inches to over 19 feet.

You should, however, find it fairly easy to recognize the trail of a lizard-like creature. Portions of the low-slung belly and tail usually drag along the surface it's walking on, and the five-toed feet alternate, rather than fall side by side, distinguishing the tracks from those left by other animals. At times, the waving tail may brush away some details of the footprints. Turtles sometimes leave similar trails, but a turtle with the same size feet as a lizard would usually leave a wider trail, with footprints closer together.

The straddle and gait of lizards vary widely depending on their size, of course; the illustration represents a lizard of about 8 inches, nose to tail tip.

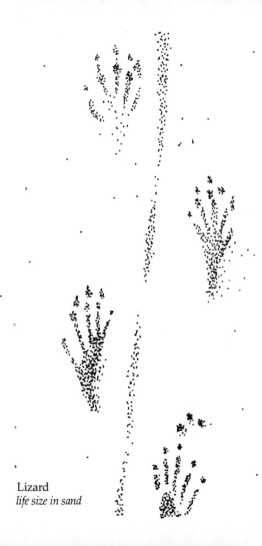

Lizard
life size in sand

STRIPED SKUNK *Mephitis mephitis*

Order: Carnivora (flesh-eating mammals). **Family:** Mustelidae (weasels and skunks). **Range and habitat:** throughout all southern states; in semi-open country, mixed woods, brushland, and open fields. **Size and weight:** 24 inches; 10 pounds. **Diet:** omnivorous, including mice, eggs, insects, grubs, fruit, carrion. **Sounds:** usually silent.

Often found dead along highways, this cat-sized skunk is easily recognized by the two broad stripes running the length of its back, meeting at head and shoulders to form a cap. A thin white stripe runs down its face. Active year round, it is chiefly nocturnal but may be sighted shortly after sunset or at dawn, snuffling around for food. It seeks shelter beneath buildings as well as in ground burrows or other protected den sites, and protects itself, when threatened, with a fine spray of extremely irritating methyl mercaptan; everyone knows what that smells like.

Striped skunk tracks are similar to but larger than those of the smaller spotted skunk, and its elongated heel pads are more often apparent because it's not as quick, agile, or highstrung as its smaller cousin. With five closely spaced toes and claws on all feet usually leaving marks, its tracks can't be mistaken for any others of its size; the spacing is distinctive, too: generally less than six inches between track groups, whether they consist of walking pairs or strung-out loping groups of four tracks.

Striped Skunk
life size in mud

VIRGINIA OPOSSUM   *Didelphis virginiana*

Order: Marsupialia (pouched mammals). **Family:** Didelphiidae. **Range and habitat:** throughout all southern states; in woodlands and adjoining areas, and farmlands, generally remaining near streams and lakes; also common around human habitations. **Size and weight:** 25 inches; 12 pounds. **Diet:** this opportunistic omnivore prefers fruits, vegetables, insects, small mammals, birds, eggs, carrion; also garbage and pet food. **Sounds:** a gurgling hiss when annoyed.

On one hand, the generally nocturnal opossum appears fairly ordinary: it looks like a large, long-haired rat, with pointed nose, pale-gray fur, and a long, scaly, reptilian tail. Primarily terrestrial, the opossum may nest in an abandoned burrow or a fallen tree, but will climb to escape danger. Other than climbing, its only defense mechanism is an ability to feign death, or "play possum."

In many respects, however, the opossum is the most peculiar animal residing on this continent. Among the oldest and most primitive of all living mammals, it is the only animal in North America with a prehensile (grasping) tail, the only nonprimate in the animal kingdom with an opposable (thumblike) digit (the inside toes on the hind feet), and the only marsupial on the continent. As many as 14 young are born prematurely after only 13 days of gestation, weighing 1/15 ounce each (the whole litter would fit into a teaspoon!). The tiny babies crawl into their mother's pouch, where they remain for the next two months. After emerging from the pouch, they often ride around on the mother's back for some time. All of this is pretty unusual behavior.

Opossums leave easily identifiable tracks: the opposable hind thumb usually points 90 degrees or more away from the direction of travel, and the five front toes spread widely. Like raccoons, opossums leave tracks in a row of pairs. Each pair consists of one front- and one rear-foot imprint, always close to or slightly overlapping each other, and the pairs are from 5 to 11 inches apart, depending on size and speed. The opossum's long tail frequently leaves drag marks on soft surfaces.

Virginia Opossum
life size in mud

WOODCHUCK
Groundhog, marmot

Marmota monax

Order: Rodentia (gnawing mammals). **Family:** Sciuridae (squirrels). **Range and habitat:** Virginia, Kentucky, Arkansas, Tennessee, and parts of north Mississippi, Alabama, Georgia, and western North and Southern Carolina; in open woods, meadows, fields, pastureland, also brushy, rocky ravines and along stream courses; a very adaptable animal. **Size and weight:** 22 inches; 8 pounds. **Diet:** almost any tender, succulent vegetation available. **Sounds:** loud, shrill chirps and whistles, especially when alarmed.

With a day set aside in February for us to concern ourselves with whether or not groundhogs see their shadows, these animals have become quite familiar. You may have seen the short-legged, plump, brown woodchuck alongside a highway, grazing and seemingly oblivious to passing traffic, or on the pavement, where its obliviousness has led it to Oblivion. Or you may have discovered one of its extensive burrows, with two or more entrances, in your lawn. The woodchuck, active during the day and hibernating during the winter, leads a solitary life but is not particularly shy of human activity.

In the absence of highway or lawn grass, woodchucks seem to like to wander along stream courses, seeking the succulent plants that flourish in such environs. On firm mud, you more than likely will find tracks like those on the right, with distinct claw and heel-pad impressions. On softer mud or wet spring snow, the tracks will look more like the two on the left. Because of their size and squirrel-family characteristics, you're not likely to mistake woodchuck tracks for anything else, but walking strides of about 3 inches and rare leaps of not more than 15 to 18 inches will verify the identity of this easygoing woodland creature.

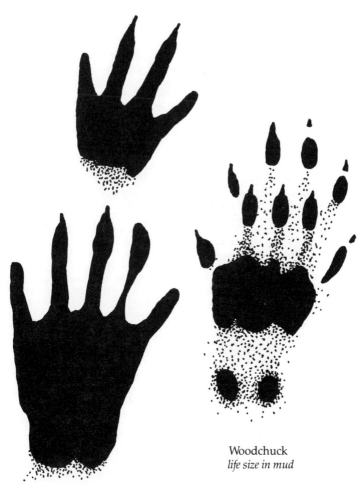

Woodchuck
life size in mud

EASTERN COTTONTAIL   *Sylvilagus floridanus*

Order: Lagomorpha (rabbitlike mammals). **Family:** Leporidae (hares and rabbits). **Range and habitat:** throughout all southern states; in dense brush and weed patches along edges of forest or swamp, with open areas nearby. **Size and weight:** 13 inches; 3 pounds. **Diet:** green vegetation, bark, twigs, sagebrush, and juniper berries. **Sounds:** usually silent; loud squeal when extremely distressed.

Cottontails are the pudgy, adorable rabbits with cottonball tails, known to us all from childhood tales of Peter Rabbit. Active day and night, year round, they're generally plentiful due in part to the fact that each adult female produces three or four litters of four to seven young rabbits every year. Of course, a variety of predators helps control their numbers, and few live more than a year in the wild.

Other family members within the southern region include the similar-sized marsh rabbit, living in moist areas from southern Alabama and Florida northeast to southeast Virginia, and the larger swamp rabbit, found in the lowland swamps of Arkansas, Louisiana, Mississippi, Alabama, north Georgia and west Tennessee.

Rabbit tracks are easily recognized because the basic pattern doesn't vary much, regardless of the rabbit's speed. It's important to note that sometimes the front feet land together, side by side, but just as often the second fore foot lands in line ahead of the first. The track clusters span 5 and 12 inches normally, with up to 3 feet between running clusters. Patient field work is the only practical way to differentiate between the tracks of these southern cottontails, where their ranges overlap.

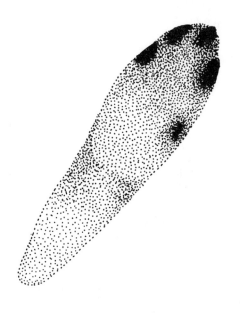

Eastern Cottontail
life size in snow

BOBCAT
Wildcat, bay lynx

Felis rufus

Order: Carnivora (flesh-eating mammals). **Family:** Felidae (cats). **Range and habitat:** throughout portions of all southern states; in forests and swamp fringes. **Size and weight:** 30 inches; 35 pounds. **Diet:** small mammals and birds; rarely carrion. **Sounds:** less vocal than the lynx, but capable of generic cat-family range of noises.

The bobcat is a very adaptable feline, afield both day and night and wandering as much as 50 miles in a day of hunting, occasionally into suburban areas. It is primarily a ground hunter, but will climb trees and drop onto unexpecting prey if the opportunity presents itself. You could mistake it for a large tabby cat with a bobbed tail, but the similarity ends there, for the bobcat has quite a wild disposition combined with much greater size, strength and razor-sharp claws and teeth.

You can expect to encounter bobcat tracks almost anywhere. You'll know the roundish tracks belong to a cat because the retractile claws never leave imprints and the toes usually spread a bit more than a dog's. Bobcat tracks are too large to be mistaken for those of a domestic cat, however. The animal's weight will have set the tracks deeper in a soft surface than you would expect from a housecat, and domestic cats have pads that are single-lobed at the front end. Bobcat tracks are clearly smaller than those of a lynx and are therefore easily identifiable by process of elimination. Similar or slightly larger tracks in western Louisiana or southwest Arkansas, however, may have been left by an ocelot. This uncommon, visually-striking cat, whose coat is covered with black-bordered brown spots, leaves tracks generally larger and less scalloped on the front and rear edges of the heel pads than those of a bobcat.

Bobcat
life size in mud

OCELOT

Felis pardalis

Order: Carnivora (flesh-eating mammals). **Family:** Felidae (cats). **Range and habitat:** southwest Arkansas and western Louisiana; in forested or brushy areas. **Size and weight:** 45 inches; 30 pounds. **Diet:** rabbits, rats, mice, birds, snakes, lizards, fish, frogs, nearly any small or young wild or domestic mammals. **Sounds:** variety of wild cat-like noises, from growls to screams.

The ocelot is a bobcat-sized animal with a proportionally smaller head and longer tail, and a visually striking coat of tawny fur with a dense pattern of black-rimmed brown spots similar to those of the jaguar but tending to form lines from shoulders to rear haunches. The ocelot is endangered; fairly rare, generally nocturnal and silent, it is difficult to sight over its limited range. It climbs and swims well, and occasionally travels and hunts in pairs, which can give a valuable clue to track identification.

Recognizing ocelot tracks, however—if you are lucky enough to find them—should not be much of a problem. The tracks have easily recognized feline characteristics, with clear heel and four well-spaced toe prints, and claw prints always absent. Although both bobcat and cougar ranges overlap the ocelot's and they share similar habitats, the ocelot's tracks are easy enough to identify: the tracks of an adult ocelot are slightly larger and wider than those of a bobcat, and clearly smaller than those left by a mountain lion. Also, the front and rear edges of the ocelot's heel pads lack the deep indentations of the bobcat's.

Ocelot
life size in mud

GRAY FOX
RED FOX

Urocyon cinereoargenteus
Vulpes vulpes

Order: Carnivora (flesh-eating mammals). **Family:** Canidae (dogs). **Range and habitat:** throughout all southern states; in varied habitats, the gray fox generally more common in wooded and brushy areas, the red fox more common in fields and farmlands. **Size and weight:** 42 inches; 12 pounds. **Diet:** omnivorous, including small mammals, birds, insects, eggs, fruit, nuts, grains, and other forage. **Sounds:** normally silent; occasionally short barking yips.

The gray fox with its gray back, rusty flanks, and white underside is generally more nocturnal and secretive than the red fox, but you might spot either one foraging by daylight in thick foliage or forested areas. The only canine in America with the ability to climb, the gray fox frequently seeks refuge and food in trees, but cottontails are the mainstay of its diet when they are available. The gray fox typically dens among boulders on the slopes of rocky ridges or in rock piles, hollow logs, or the like; unlike the red fox, it uses these dens in winter as well as summer.

Gray fox tracks are very similar to those of the red fox, except that the prints are usually more distinct due to the relative lack of fur on the animal's feet. The tracks of both foxes always show the imprints of claws; gray fox tracks may be the same size or slightly smaller and narrower than the red fox's, with 8 to 18 inches between walking prints. Both foxes tend to leave a line of single tracks, spaced farther apart than those of a domestic dog of similar foot size, with a trail width of 3–4 inches.

Gray Fox
life size in mud

RACCOON
Coon

Procyon lotor

Order: Carnivora (flesh-eating mammals). **Family:** Procyonidae (raccoons, ringtails, and coatis). **Range and habitat:** throughout all southern states; in forest fringes and rocky areas near streams, ponds, and lakes. **Size and weight:** 36 inches; 25 pounds. **Diet:** omnivorous, including fish, amphibians, shellfish, insects, birds, eggs, mice, carrion, berries, nuts, and vegetation. **Sounds:** a variety of shrill cries, whistles, churrs, growls, and screeches.

From childhood most of us know the raccoon by its mask of black fur and its black tail stripes on an otherwise grayish-brown body. It's familiar as a character in kids' books and frontier lore, frequently seen as a road kill, and is both curious and bold enough to be a fairly common visitor to campgrounds and even residential homes nearly everywhere within its range. Chiefly nocturnal, raccoons are more commonly sighted in suburban neighborhoods raiding garbage cans and terrorizing family hounds than in wildlands. Interesting and intelligent animals with manual dexterity of great renown, raccoons are also reputed to make lively and intriguing pets, provided they are closely supervised.

Raccoons like to wash or tear food items apart in water, which apparently improves their manual sensitivity. Much of their food comes from aquatic prospecting, so you will often find their tracks near water. When a raccoon walks, its left rear foot is placed next to the right front foot, and so forth, forming paired track clusters. Running-track clusters tend to be bunched irregularly. The walking stride of a raccoon is about 7 inches; leaps average 20 inches.

Raccoon
life size in mud

COYOTE
Brush wolf, prairie wolf

Canis latrans

Order: Carnivora (flesh-eating mammals). **Family:** Canidae (dogs). **Range and habitat:** portions of Arkansas, Kentucky, Tennessee, North Carolina, Louisiana, Mississippi, and Georgia; primarily in open woodlands and brushy fringes, but very adaptable; can turn up anywhere. **Size and weight:** 48 inches; 45 pounds. **Diet:** omnivorous, including rodents and other small mammals, fish, carrion, insects, berries, grains, nuts, and vegetation. **Sounds:** wide range of canine sounds; most often heard yelping in group chorus late at night.

An important controller of small rodents, the smart, adaptable coyote is—unlike the gray wolf—steadily expanding its range. About the size of a collie, the coyote is a good runner and swimmer and has great stamina. Despite its wide range, it is shy, and you will be lucky to see one in the wild.

Typically canine, the coyote's front paw is slightly larger than the rear, and the front toes tend to spread wider, though not as wide as the bobcat's. The toenails nearly always leave imprints. The shape of coyote pads is unique, the front pads differing markedly from the rear, as shown, and the outer toes are usually slightly larger than the inner toes on each foot. The coyote tends to walk in a straight line and keep its tail down, which often leaves an imprint in deep snow. These characteristics plus walking strides of 8 to 16 inches, trail width of 4–6 inches, and leaps to 10 feet may help you distinguish coyote tracks from those of domestic dogs with feet of the same size.

Coyote
life size in mud

RED WOLF

Canis rufus

Order: Carnivora (flesh-eating mammals). **Family:** Canidae (dogs). **Range and habitat:** southwest Louisiana; in forested or brushy areas, coastal plains, swamps and bayous. **Size and weight:** 60 inches; 65 pounds. **Diet:** primarily rabbits, also small or young animals, birds, and crabs along the Gulf Coast of Louisiana. **Sounds:** variety of dog-family noises and music, often a clear, high tremolo chorus on moonlit nights.

The red wolf usually looks and acts like a large coyote with a finely mottled grayish-red coat, although black, brown, yellowish and gray specimens have also been seen; a great variety of size and color can be expected, because the red wolf interbreeds readily with the coyote. In fact, since the red wolf's range is wholly overlapped by the coyote, this uncommon southwestern wolf may be doomed to exterminate itself through hybridization. Like the coyote, the red wolf is largely nocturnal and, although little is actually known of its habits, it is said to run with its tail up, whereas the coyote keeps its tail down. With patience and the mouse-squeak made by kissing the back of your hand, you can sometimes lure canines in for precise identification.

Without an actual sighting it will be difficult to positively identify red wolf tracks because, well, who can say if the tracks were left by a large coyote, a small red wolf, or any of numerous hybrid offspring? Generally speaking, the red wolf's tracks are larger than the coyote's and the outer toes are slightly smaller than the middle toes. If track length is longer than 3 inches, and there are no tail-drag marks on soft surfaces, the trail is likely that of the elusive red wolf.

Red Wolf
1/2 life size in mud

RIVER OTTER
Land otter

Lutra canadensis

Order: Carnivora (flesh-eating mammals). **Family:** Mustelidae (the weasel family). **Range and habitat:** throughout all southern states; in and near lakes and streams. **Size and weight:** 48 inches; 25 pounds. **Diet:** fish, amphibians, shellfish and other aquatic invertebrates, snakes, turtles, birds, eggs. **Sounds:** chirps, chatters, chuckles, grunts, and growls.

The river otter is a dark brown weasel about as large as a medium-sized dog, with a thick, hairless tail adapted for swimming, much like that of the muskrat; in fact, the river otter closely resembles the muskrat in appearance and habitat, but is much larger, strictly carnivorous, and quite a bit more animated. Both in and out of water, alone or in the company of others, the river otter seems to be a graceful and exuberant playful animal. Active during the daylight hours, the otter is wary of humans. Still, you might occasionally sight one in the wild; more commonly you may find, in summer, the flattened grass where otters have rolled, leaving their musky odor behind, or in winter, marks on snow or ice where they've playfully slid on their bellies.

River otter tracks are relatively easy to find and identify within the otter's range. The webs of the rear feet often leave distinct marks on soft surfaces, and claw marks usually are present. Individual tracks measure up to 3.5 inches across and due to their size cannot be confused with those of any other animal with similar aquatic habitat. River otters do venture into woodlands as well. Otter tracks meander, forming a trail roughly 8 to 10 inches wide and generally leading to or from water systems. Also, the river otter normally leaves groups of four tracks 13 to 30 inches apart, when it's not sliding on its belly.

River Otter
life size in mud

WHITE-TAILED DEER
Whitetail, Virginia deer

Odocoileus virginianus

Order: Artiodactyla (even-toed hoofed mammals). **Family:** Cervidae (deer). **Range and habitat:** throughout all southern states; in deciduous and mixed woodlands, nearby meadows, river bottomlands, creeksides, open brushy areas, and swamp fringes. **Height and weight:** 42 inches at shoulder; 250 pounds. **Diet:** browse from shrubs and lower tree limbs; less frequently fungi, nuts, grains, grasses, and herbs. **Sounds:** low bleats, guttural grunts, snorts, and whistles of alarm.

The white-tailed deer is recognizable by the all-white underside of its tail, which the animal raises prominently when it runs. It has a home range of only a square mile or so, although some migrate to swamps in cold weather. White-tailed deer usually gather in groups of no more than 3 animals, except in the dead of winter when the group may swell to 25. They spend their days browsing and quietly chewing their cuds and when startled run only short distances to the nearest cover.

The white-tailed deer's range overlaps that of the elk, but its tracks are smaller. Individual deer tracks are relatively long and slender, averaging about 3 inches in length; the dewclaws will leave prints in snow or soft earth. When running, the white-tailed deer tends to trot, often leaving tracks in a more or less straight line, with up to 6 feet between track groups. Its walking gait is less than 20 inches, with tracks frequently doubled up, as the rear feet cover prints left by the front. A few herds of elk inhabit upland portions of southwestern Virginia and northern Arkansas. Elk tracks average about 4.5 inches in length, with walking strides of 22 inches or more, so you will have no problem telling them apart.

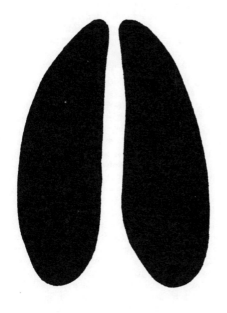

White-tailed Deer
life size in mud

WILD BOAR

Sus scrofa

Order: Artiodactyla (even-toed hoofed mammals). **Family:** Suidae (Old World swine). **Range and habitat:** portions of all southern states except Kentucky and Virginia; variable, from densely forested mountainous terrain, into adjoining brushlands, dry hills, and swampy fringes, particularly in winter. **Height and weight:** 36 inches at shoulder; 300 pounds. **Diet:** acorns and other nuts, roots, grasses, fruit, also small amphibians, eggs, occasionally small mammals and carrion. **Sounds:** grunts and squeals typical of domestic pigs.

Wild boars are strong, agile and occasionally aggressive animals that can be dangerous to encounter in the dense vegetation they tend to prefer. They were brought from Russia in 1910 to stock hunting preserves in North Carolina, where some inevitably escaped and bred with feral domestic pigs, so that today America's wild boars are largely hybrids. These brown or gray creatures are recognizably piglike in shape but their humped backs, shaggy coats, and formidable tusks readily distinguish them from domestic animals. They are most active at dawn and dusk, are good swimmers and fast runners, and usually move about in family groups of 6 or so animals but occasionally congregate in herds of up to 50.

Their tracks could be mistaken for those of the white-tailed deer, which overlap their range, but note that wild boar tracks are more rounded, with toes more splayed, heels together—often to the extent that no break is apparent in the imprint at all—and dewclaw imprints, in soft ground, farther out to the sides than in deer tracks. Wild boar have strides of about 18 inches, usually in a narrow line. They root around on the ground in their search for nuts and other food, leaving behind characteristic diggings and tusk gouge marks within three feet of the ground. Deer, on the other hand, leave narrower hoofprints with heels usually separated, 20-inch strides, and evidence of browsing foliage five or six feet above the ground surface.

Wild Boar
life size in mud

MOUNTAIN LION
Puma, cougar, panther, catamount

Felis concolor

Order: Carnivora (flesh-eating mammals). **Family:** Felidae (cats). **Range and habitat:** portions of Arkansas, Louisiana, Mississippi, Alabama, the Smoky Mountains, and south Florida; in remote, isolated mountains, forests, and swamp fringes. **Size and weight:** 84 inches; 200 pounds. **Diet:** primarily deer, small mammals, and birds; occasionally domestic animals. **Sounds:** generally quiet, but capable of a variety of voluminous feline screams, hisses, and growls.

Hunted to the verge of extinction, our large, tawny, native American cat with its long, waving tail is now so scarce and secretive and is confined to such remote terrain that you'd be very lucky to sight one in the wild. But you at least have a chance to find the tracks of this big cat, which hunts mostly on the ground. It occasionally climbs trees, particularly to evade dogs but also to drop onto unwary prey (the mountain lion is an important natural control of the deer population).

Mountain lion tracks are significantly larger than those of either of the two smaller cats, the bobcat and the ocelot, that share parts of its range. Spacing of tracks will also be what you'd expect of the large cat: trail width of 12 inches or more, walking tracks over 20 inches apart, 3 feet separating pairs of loping tracks, and bounding leaps of 12 feet or more. Another sure sign is the tail drag marks that may be found, especially in snow. Of course, like all cats, the mountain lion has retractile claws, which never leave marks.

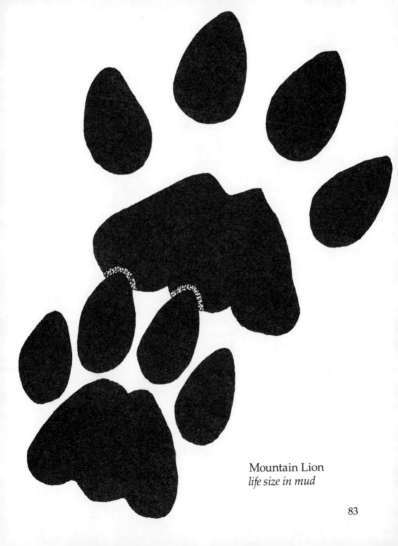

Mountain Lion
life size in mud

83

SNOWSHOE HARE
Varying hare

Lepus americanus

Order: Lagomorpha (rabbitlike mammals). **Family:** Leporidae (hares and rabbits). **Range and habitat:** mountainous portions of southwest Virginia, western North Carolina, east Tennessee and east Kentucky; in upland forests, brush thickets, and swamp fringes. **Size and weight:** 18 inches; 4 pounds. **Diet:** succulent vegetation in summer, twigs, bark, and buds in winter; occasionally eats frozen meat. **Sounds:** generally silent; may thump feet, scream, grunt, or groan occasionally.

This medium-sized member of the rabbit family is active day and night year round and quite common over a large territory within its preferred habitat. The animal has two color phases: medium brown in summer months, molting in winter to white—sometimes slightly mottled with brown—with black ear tips. Aptly named, its unique heavily furred hind feet have separable toes, allowing them to function like snowshoes when the hare is traveling on soft surfaces, especially deep snow.

Although its range partially overlaps that of the eastern cottontail, track recognition is easy because of the natural snowshoe formed by its toes. A snowshoe hare's toes always spread out, leaving distinctively separate imprints. The length of each track cluster of four prints average 11 inches; hopping distance is about 14 inches with leaps of more than 5 feet.

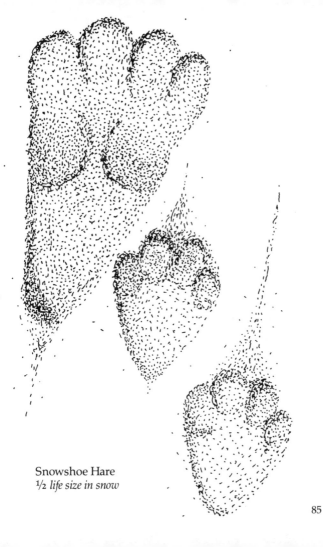

Snowshoe Hare
1/2 life size in snow

BEAVER

Castor canadensis

Order: Rodentia (gnawing mammals). **Family:** Castoridae (beavers). **Range and habitat:** widespread throughout all southern states except most of Florida; in marshes, streams and lakes with brush and trees, or in open forest along riverbanks. **Size and weight:** 36 inches; 55 pounds. **Diet:** aquatic plants, bark, and the twigs and leaves of many shrubs and trees, preferably alder, cottonwood, and willow. **Sounds:** nonvocal, but smacks tail on water surface quite loudly to signal danger.

This industrious, aquatic mammal is the largest North American rodent. Although it sometimes lives unobtrusively in a riverbank, usually it constructs the familiar beaver lodge, a roughly conical pile of brush, stones, and mud extending as much as 6 feet above the surface of a pond, and gnaws down dozens of small softwood trees with which it constructs a conspicuous system of dams, often several hundred yards long. A beaver can grasp objects with its front paws and stand and walk upright on its hind feet. It uses its flat, scaly, strong tail for support out of water and as a rudder when swimming. Gregarious animals, beavers work well together on their collective projects. They are active day and night year round, but may operate unobserved beneath the ice, where present, during much of the winter, using subsurface lodge entrances.

If you are lucky, the large, webbed hind foot tracks left by a beaver will be clear, with 6 to 8 inches between pairs. Beavers frequently, however, obscure part or most of their tracks by dragging their tails and/or branches over them, leaving a trail much like that of a 6-inch-wide turtle, except the beaver's tail-drag trail zigzags slightly every 6 or 8 inches. The zigzag is the key to identification, as a turtle moves in reasonably long, straight segments until it changes direction significantly.

Beaver
½ life size in mud

BLACK BEAR

Ursus americanus

Order: Carnivora (flesh-eating mammals). **Family:** Ursidae (bears). **Range and habitat:** parts of Arkansas, western Virginia south through the Appalachians, south Louisiana and most of Florida; forests and swamp fringes. **Size and weight:** 78 inches; 450 pounds. **Diet:** omnivorous, including smaller mammals, fish, carrion, insects, fruit, berries, nuts, and succulent plants. **Sounds:** usually silent, but may growl, grunt, woof, whimper, click teeth, smack jaws together, or make other immediately recognizable indications of annoyance or alarm.

The black bear is the smallest and most common American bear. You may have seen these animals around rural garbage dumps and in parks. In the wild, the black bear is shy and wary of human contact as a general rule and thus not frequently sighted. If you do sight one, however, it can be very dangerous to underestimate it. The black bear is very strong, agile, and quick. It climbs trees, swims well, can run 25 miles per hour for short stretches, and above all else, is unpredictable. The black bear may seem docile and harmless in parks, but it has been known to chase people with great determination, even going so far as to swim in pursuit of a retreating floatplane, and there are many recorded examples to prove the black bear's fondness for human flesh.

Be alert for bear trails, worn deep by generations of bears, and for trees with claw marks and other indications of bear territory. Bear tracks are usually easy to identify; they are roughly human in shape and size but slightly wider. The large claws leave prints wherever the toes do. If a bear slips on mud or ice, its soles leave distinctive smooth slide marks; nearby you will no doubt find more orderly tracks. Adult black bear tracks measure about 7 inches.

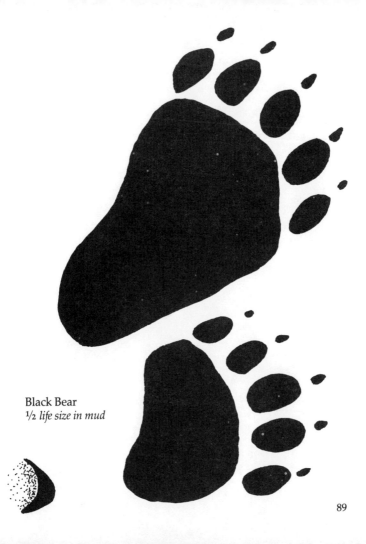

Black Bear
½ life size in mud

89

Birds

CARDINAL

Richmondena cardinalis

Order: Passeriformes (perching birds). **Family:** Fringillidae (buntings, finches, and sparrows). **Range and habitat:** year-round resident throughout southern states; common in and near suburbs, weedy fields, brushy forest fringes. **Size and weight:** length 8 inches, wingspan 12 inches; less than 1 ounce. **Diet:** seeds, insects, and berries. **Sounds:** repetitive loud slurred whistles.

The cardinal, a common and wide-ranging little bird, is our only southern crested bird with a conical beak. The bright red male with the black throat is unmistakable, but the yellow-brown female is also easy to identify because of her pointed crest and thick beak. The cardinal is a common suburban visitor and easily attracted to feeders.

Cardinal tracks are typical of the vast number of smaller land birds that leave delicate lines on snow, sand, or mud of inland areas. Hind toes are about twice as long as front toes, and the tracks are found in pairs spaced up to 7 inches apart, as these birds hop instead of walk. The relative size of the tracks will give a clue to the identity of the maker, as will habitat and seasonal considerations, verified, of course, by actual field sightings.

Cardinal
life size in snow

NORTHERN FLICKER

Colaptes auratus

Order: Piciformes (woodpeckers and allies). **Family:** Picidae. **Range and habitat:** year-round resident throughout the southern states; in open country near large trees. **Size and weight:** length, 10 inches; wingspan, 14 inches; weight, 4 ounces. **Diet:** insects. **Sounds:** loud repeated flick or flicker, also shrill descending kee-oo.

Widespread and common, the flicker is most easily recognized by the black polka-dots on its white chest and belly, and the yellow or orange plumage under its wings. These jay-sized woodpeckers often fly down to the ground to eat ants and other insects and grubs.

A variety of other woodpeckers and the yellow-bellied sapsucker visit or reside in the southern region; all have feet of the same distinctive shape, adapted for clinging to tree trunks and limbs while the birds dig for wood-boring insects, but they rarely leave the trees, so when you find tracks like those illustrated, you can feel reasonably sure they were left by a ground-visiting flicker.

Northern Flicker
life size in mud

KILLDEER

Charadrius vociferus

Order: Charadriiformes (shorebirds, gulls, and terns). **Family:** Charadriidae (plovers). **Range and habitat:** year-round resident in most of southern states but summer resident only in the Appalachians; common along shorelines, also found on inland fields and pastures. **Size and weight:** length 8 inches, wingspan 12 inches; 4 ounces. **Diet:** insects and larvae, earthworms, seeds. **Sounds:** repeats its name as its call.

The killdeer is one of the most common and recognizable shorebirds. Its two black breast bands are distinctive, as is its habit of feigning injury to lead intruders away from its nesting area. The killdeer is the only shorebird found year round in most of the region. Its tracks are typical as well of the tracks—usually found on damp sand—of shorebirds that visit the Southeast seasonally: the front center toe is longer than the two outer toes; the small hind toe, more of a heel spur than a toe, leaves a small imprint; and the tracks are usually printed in a line, only an inch or two apart for birds the size of the killdeer, less for sandpipers, and up to 6 inches for birds the size of a greater yellowlegs. The general shape and lack of any evidence of webbing between the toes separate shorebird tracks from those of gulls or ducks.

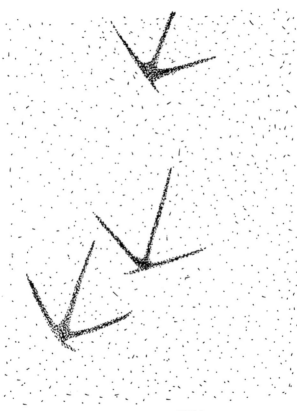

Killdeer
life size in sand

AMERICAN CROW

Corvus brachyrhynchos

Order: Passeriformes (perching birds). **Family:** Corvidae (jays, magpies, crows). **Range and habitat:** year-round resident throughout the southern states; in all habitats. **Size and weight:** length 17 inches, wingspan 26 inches; 1 pound. **Diet:** nearly everything from mice to carrion to garbage. **Sounds:** distinctive "caw."

Crows are relatively intelligent birds, quite vocal, make good pets and can be taught to mimic human voices. Researchers have also determined that crows can count, and both wild and pet crows have been observed making up games to play. Watching crows will often help you locate other wildlife, too: groups of crows will mob and scold a predator such as an owl, for example, or perch near an offensive animal, darting in to harass and scold it. The common crow can be told from a distant hawk by its frequent steady flapping; it seldom glides more than 2 or 3 seconds except in strong updrafts or when descending.

All four of the crow's toes are about the same length, each with a strong claw, all of which leave prints most of the time. Crows walk and skip; their tracks are not usually made in pairs.

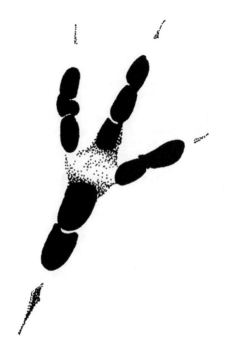

American Crow
life size in mud

MALLARD
Anas platyrhynchos

Order: Anseriformes. **Family:** Anatidae (ducks, geese and swans). **Range and habitat:** winter or year-round resident of the southern states; in shallow coastal waters as well as in lakes, ponds, and freshwater marshes. **Size and weight:** length 28 inches, wingspan 40 inches; 3.5 pounds. **Diet:** grains, insects, and small aquatic plants, mollusks and fish. **Sounds:** a loud quack.

The mallard, the most common surface-feeding duck in most of the Southeast, is easily recognized by its blue speculum (wing band) with a visible white border and particularly the green head, white neck band, and rusty breast of the male. Mallards are usually seen in the wild, dabbling and tipping in water shallows, but they are not shy around humans and are often found waiting patiently for handouts around park ponds, waterfront cafes, and similar civilized habitat. In water they rarely dive; in flight they are agile and take off at a steep angle.

The tracks are typical of all waterfowl, as well as coastal birds including all seagulls, cormorants, terns, shearwaters, petrels, gannets, pelicans and jaegers. All these birds have hind toes so small and elevated that they do not leave imprints. The three main toes fan out in front and are connected by webs, which nearly always leave prints. Tracks like these will range in size from somewhat less than 2 inches long for small ducks to 7 inches for pelicans. Once again, with tracks as initial clues, patient field work and an intimate knowledge of the species frequenting the area at the time of year the tracks are found will allow you to accurately guess the track maker's identity.

Mallard
life size in mud

GREAT BLUE HERON   *Ardea herodias*

Order: Ciconiiformes (herons and allies). **Family:** Ardeidae (herons, egrets, and bitterns). **Range and habitat:** year-round resident of lowland areas, spring or summer only in the Appalachians; in most lowland areas, common on freshwater and ocean shores. **Size and weight:** length 48 inches, wingspan 72 inches; 7 pounds. **Diet:** fish, snakes, insects, mice, and frogs. **Sounds:** "kraak" and strident honks.

The presence of a great blue heron magically transforms an aquatic landscape, adding an aura of quiet elegance characteristic of the best Oriental brush paintings. This large heron typically walks slowly through shallows or stands with head hunched on shoulders, looking for the fish that make up a large part of its diet. A heron's nest, maintained year after year, is an elaborate structure of sticks 3 feet across built in a tree; great blue herons often nest colonially.

You will most often find great blue heron tracks bordering the freshwater areas where the bird feeds. The four toes and claws of each foot usually leave visible imprints. The well-developed hind toe enables the heron to stand for long periods of time on one leg or the other or to walk very slowly while hunting.

This track shape is typical of all the herons, egrets, bitterns, ibises, spoonbills, gallinules, coots, cranes, and rails found in the southern states. The size and location of the tracks will vary according to species.

Great Blue Heron
life size in mud

GREAT HORNED OWL
Cat owl

Bubo virginianus

Order: Strigiformes (owls). **Family:** Strigidae (owls). **Range and habitat:** widespread throughout all southern states year round; in most habitats. **Size and weight:** length 24 inches, wingspan 48 inches; 3.5 pounds. **Diet:** rabbits, mice, rats, voles, skunks, and grouse. **Sounds:** males normally hoot four or five times in sequence, females six to eight times.

This common, large, "eared" owl does look catlike when it sits staring at you from a lofty perch or nesting tree. The male and female prefer to use nests constructed in previous years by hawks or ravens rather than building their own, and they nest so early in spring that the brooding female is often partially covered with snow, where snow occurs. Special modifications of its wing feathers allow this night hunter to drop silently onto the back of unsuspecting prey.

The shape of the tracks illustrated is representative of numerous species of owls inhabiting the southern region. Owl tracks are uncommon except in snow country, where an owl may leave a few tracks around a kill site or when it lands to investigate and feed on food too heavy to carry away. You may also find owl tracks on recently rained-upon dirt roads where an owl has discovered a car-killed animal.

The tracks of the great horned owl in mud show its three thick, powerful toes and imprints of its long, sharp talons. The hind toe mark is always insignificant or absent. Smaller owl species obviously leave smaller tracks. Unless you are lucky enough to see these smaller owls in the act of making tracks, there's no way to identify the tracks by species. You might get a clue by observing the area at dusk, the best time for sighting owls, to see what species are present in the vicinity of the tracks you have found.

Great Horned Owl
life size in mud

105

Recommended Reading

CARE OF THE WILD FEATHERED AND FURRED: A Guide to Wildlife Handling and Care, Mae Hickman and Maxine Guy (Unity Press, 1973); unique perspectives on animal behavior and emergency care of injured and orphaned wildlife.

A FIELD GUIDE TO ANIMAL TRACKS, Olaus J. Murie (Houghton Mifflin Co., Boston, 2nd ed., 1975); a classic work on track identification by Murie (1889–1963), an eminent naturalist and wildlife artist; one of the Peterson Field Guide Series; an excellent research text for home study.

ISLAND SOJOURN, Elizabeth Arthur (Harper & Row, 1980); an account of life on an island in British Columbia's wilderness, with a chapter devoted to a metaphysical perspective of animal tracks.

SNOW TRACKS, Jean George (E. P. Dutton, 1958); an introduction to the study of animal tracks for very young children.

THE TRACKER, Tom Brown and William J. Watkins (Berkley Publications, 1984); an intriguing story by a man who has devoted his life to the science of following tracks and other movement clues of various animals, including humans.

Index

About the author:

Chris Stall first became interested in wild country and wild animals during several years with a very active Boy Scout troop in rural New York State, where he spent his youth. In the two decades since then he has travelled and lived around most of North America, studying, photographing, sketching and writing about wild animals in their natural habitats. His photos and articles have appeared in a number of outdoor and nature magazines. Stall currently lives in Cincinnati, his launching point for a 1365-mile solo kayak journey down the Mississippi River to New Orleans in 1988.

Look for these other "natural items" from The Mountaineers:

MAC'S FIELD GUIDES
This series of plastic laminated cards can be easily fit in a pack, taped to a kayak deck, dropped in the sand, marked with crayons or grease pencil and still keep on giving great information. Developed by a teacher of marine science, these field guides have color drawings to readily identify a wide array of wildlife, complete with both common and scientific names, and information on size and habitat. Each card: $4.95

FRESHWATER FISH OF NORTH AMERICA
MARINE MAMMALS OF NORTH AMERICA
NORTHEAST COASTAL BIRDS
NORTHEAST COASTAL INVERTEBRATES
NORTHWEST COASTAL FISH
NORTHWEST COASTAL INVERTEBRATES
SOUTHWEST COASTAL FISH
WATER BIRDS OF THE NORTHWEST COAST

At your book, nature or outdoor store, or order direct from the publisher. Order toll-free with VISA / MasterCard—1-800-553-4453—or send check or money order. Add $2.00 per order for shipping and handling. Ask for complete catalog.

THE MOUNTAINEERS
306 2nd Ave. W.
Seattle, WA   98119

Collect ANIMAL TRACKS books and posters for other regions of the country!

For your own travels, or for gifts to friends and relatives in other regions, look for these fine books and matching posters at your nearby book, nature or out-door stores, or order direct from the publisher.

BOOKS are all the same size and format as the one you hold in your hand, ready for pocket, pack or glove compartment. $4.95 each.

POSTERS are large (25" × 38"), top-quality, two-color posters richly printed on heavy stock. Each shows most of the same 40–50 tracks from the matching book. Every poster is a different color for display as a set. $5.95 each.

Areas available:

GREAT LAKES	PACIFIC NORTHWEST
MID-ATLANTIC	ROCKY MOUNTAINS
NEW ENGLAND	CALIFORNIA

Order toll-free with VISA / MasterCard—1-800-553-4453—or send check or money order. Add $2.00 per order for shipping and handling, **plus** *$1.50 if your order includes a poster:*

THE MOUNTAINEERS
306 2nd Ave. W.
Seattle, WA   98119